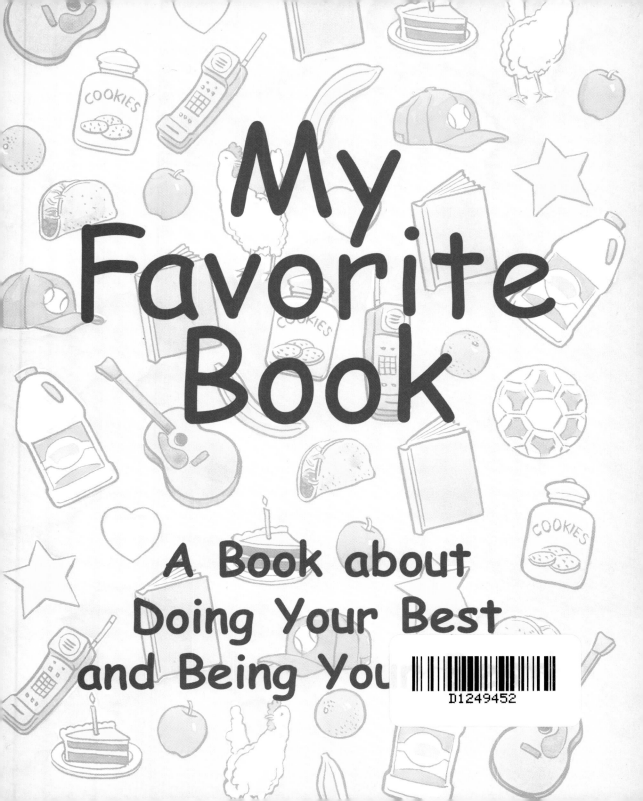

# My Favorite Book

## A Book about Doing Your Best and Being You

# This is
# My Favorite Book.

## This is the way I look.

## I am _b_ years old.

## This is the way I write my name.

Tiana B weatherby

**The name of my school is**

Edgar Elementary

**The name of my teacher is**

Mrs. Nowak

**The name of my town is**

Edgar

**The name of my state is**

Wisconsin

# Acknowledgments

(The people who helped make *My Favorite Book*)

*My Favorite Book* was written by John Sydney Tighe
and illustrated by Christopher Pelicano.

Lewis Holland helped produce *My Favorite Book*
and Ron Mahannah helped design it and lay out the pages.

## Our Education Consultants

Dan Seufert, M.Ed

Mr. Dan studied Education in school and has worked in school systems since he got out of college. Over the years, he has written and presented a lot of material designed to help kids. He is a Self-Contained Teacher of Behaviorally Emotionally Disabled Children in the Charlotte-Mecklenburg, North Carolina School System.

Pamela Gabbard, M.Ed

Mrs. Pam studied Education, Counseling and Psychology when she went to college. She has always loved helping kids and has been very active in the American School Counselor Association. She is an Elementary School Counselor at Ballard County Elementary School in Barlow, Kentucky.

Special Thanks to the American School Counselor Association and to kids and parents everywhere who are trying to do their best and be their best.

# My Favorite Book

### Sponsored by

## *ALL-SEASON*

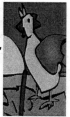

Do Your Best and Be Your Best

# America The Beautiful

# United We Stand

# Contents

# Good Manners!!!

Hi! My name is Sherri. I have good manners. I use my fork and my spoon at dinner.

I show my good manners when I say "please" and
"thank you" and when I am nice to others.

I show my good manners when I listen to the grown-ups in charge. That may be my mom or my dad or someone else who is taking care of me.

We learn good manners at home. Then we learn more good manners at school. We have to get along with our brothers and sisters, don't we? If we want good manners we have to work at it!

# Let's Talk About Respect

How do you show your good manners at home?

How do you show your good manners at school?

## What Words Mean
**Good Manners** – Having good manners is being respectful of other people. People with good manners are polite. They say "please' and "thank you." They are always willing to help their parents or their friends.

## Words To Spell
P-l-e-a-s-e
P-o-l-i-t-e

# Making The World Better!

Hi! My name is Shannon. Last summer I visited my grandma and my grandpa. They live on a farm!

Gramps and Grammy have lots of animals. They have chickens and pigs and cows, too. They grow lots of food, like beans and corn. Their corn is taller than I am! Gramps and Grammy work very hard. Did you know that farmers feed the whole world?

When I visit Gramps and Grammy, I have a job. My job is to feed the chickens. I feed them early in the morning. The chickens are always happy to see me!

Gramps and Grammy called me responsible. They said kids like me make the world better. I can make the world better just by feeding the chickens! At home I have chores, too. I do not like some of my chores, but I feel good when I finish them. Then I know I am making the world better!

# Let's Talk About Being Responsible

How do you make the world better?

What are your chores at home? How do you feel when you finish them?

## What Words Mean
**Chores** – Chores are jobs you have to do. Doing a chore well, even if you make mistakes, shows responsibility.

## Words To Spell
W-o-r-k
R-e-s-p-o-n-s-i-b-l-e

# The Hero

My name is Jeremy and some people call me a hero. I just try to do what my mom and my dad teach me!

One day at our house there was an accident. My mom was at the market. My dad was cutting the grass. All of a sudden I heard my dad yell! I ran to the door and saw my dad lying on the ground.

My dad would not wake up! I sure was scared! I ran inside our house and pressed 911 on the telephone. Someone said, "911, What's your emergency?" I said, "My dad fell down and got hurt and he won't wake up!"

The lady on the phone asked me who lived next door. I told her Mrs. Robinson lived next door. The lady was nice. She talked to me and calmed me down.

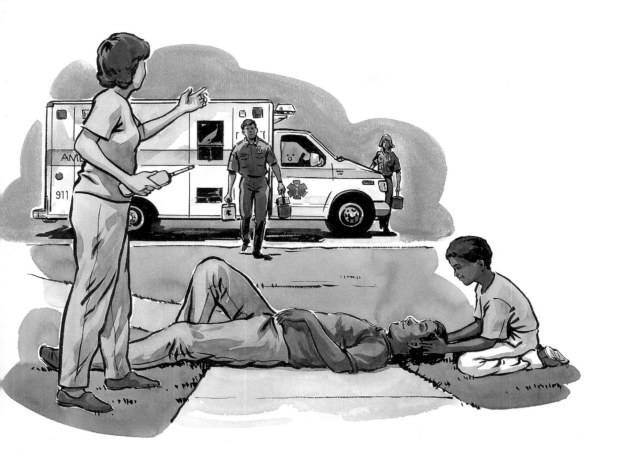

Soon Mrs. Robinson came running over. Then an ambulance came to our house. A man and a woman checked my dad. They said a rock hit his eye and made him fall down. He hit his head when he fell down. They said he was going to have a big bump on his head, and that he scratched his eye. They told me he was going to be O.K., though. That made me feel better.

The next day a man from the newspaper came to talk to me. He said I was brave. Then my picture was in the newspaper and there was a story about me. The story called me a hero! I just did what my mom and dad taught me to do.

Mom and Dad were proud of me. They said I was responsible. Since I was a hero, I thought maybe I would not have to clean my room. Mom and Dad said that was very funny! They said, "Sorry, Jeremy, even heroes have to clean their rooms!"

# Let's Talk
# About Being Brave

Can you tell about someone you know who is brave?

How do you make an emergency telephone call?

**What Words Mean**
**Being Brave** – Being brave is doing the right thing even if you are afraid.

**Words To Spell**
B-r-a-v-e
H-e-r-o

# Our Community

Can you match the people to what they do to
help our community? Write the correct number
in the right hand column or draw a line
from the people to what they do.

1. Pharmacist              ___Helps children learn their lessons

2. Firefighter             ___Helps families when they get sick

3. Police Officer          ___Helps families with their money

4. Banker                  ___Helps put out fires and helps people
                              who have been in an accident

5. Grocer                  ___Helps families buy the things they
                              need or they want

6. Mail Carrier            ___Helps people who are in trouble and
                              tries to stop people from breaking
                              the law

7. Teacher                 ___Helps families have lots of books to
                              read

8. Businessperson          ___Helps families get letters and
                              packages

9. Librarian               ___Helps families get the medicine they
                              need

10. Doctor/Nurse           ___Helps families get food

## What do you like best about your community?

# Friends

Hi! My name is Kim. These are my friends. We like each other lots! My teacher says that friends help each other. She says they are kind to each other, too.

One time a third grader made fun of me. It hurt my feelings. My friend Sydney made me feel better. I think Sydney is my best friend!

I forgot to invite my friend Holly to my birthday party. That hurt her feelings. I told Holly I was sorry. My mom said it was O.K. for Holly and her little brother Jack to come over one day after school.

We had lots of fun, but Jackie Boy hid our dolls from us! Mom says we have to be patient with little kids. Maybe Holly is my best friend, too!

# Let's Talk About Friendship

What are some fun things you do with your friends?

How do you show your friends that you care for them?

**What Words Mean**
**Friends** – Friends are people who care about each other and like to spend time with each other. They also respect each other by being honest and thoughtful.

**Words To Spell**
F-r-i-e-n-d
K-i-n-d

# My Family

Hi! My name is Bobby. My mom and my dad are from Mexico. They speak English very well and they love the United States!

My grandmother lives with us, too. We call her Abuela. Abuela is the word for grandmother in Spanish. She tells us stories about people who lived in Mexico more than five hundred years ago! She calls the stories our tradition. My grandmother is wise. I love her very much!

Tío Pepe is my papa's old friend. Tío is the word for uncle in Spanish. Tío Pepe is not really our uncle, though. We call him that because my papa says he is just like family! Tío Pepe and Papa laugh and sing together.

Pancho is our dog. He has funny hair. He likes to chew on my papa's slippers. Pancho gets into lots of trouble. But we still love him!

My mom helps me with my homework. She sings to me at bedtime. Her songs are all about love. She says love is the best thing there is! She also says love begins at home. That is why our family is so important...yes, even Pancho!

# Let's Talk About Family

How is your family like Bobby's family?

Bobby's family came from Mexico. Where did your family come from?

**What Words mean**
**Family** – Our family is our mom and dad, our brothers and sisters and all our relatives. Some of our good friends are like our family because we are close to them.

**Words To Spell**
G-r-a-n-d-m-o-t-h-e-r
L-o-v-e

# How I Got In Trouble

Hi! My name is Tommy. I got in lots of trouble after school one day. I felt really bad!

I took out some bottles under our kitchen sink. I showed the bottles to my little sister. Those bottles are poison!

The stuff in the bottles cleans our floors and our windows. If you swallowed some of it, it would hurt you!

It is against our rules to play with things like that. If I don't follow the rules Mom may not let me play on my soccer team!

Rules can keep us safe. When I break the rules or make a bad choice, it can hurt me. It is a bad choice for kids to use tobacco or alcohol. Their bodies are not going to be healthy if they do!

# Let's Talk
# About Following Rules

What are some of the rules you have at home and at school?

Can you name a rule that keeps you safe?

## What Words Mean
**Rules** – Rules are directions our parents or teachers or other grown-ups give us. Rules keep us safe.

## Words To Spell
P-o-i-s-o-n
R-u-l-e-s

# Be Good to Your Body

I like my hands and I like my feet
but when my nose stops up I can't fall asleep!
We go see the doctor if my cold gets bad
'cause colds can make you stuffy and sad.

My fingers work fine when they point or write
but sometimes they spill everything in sight!
Mom says don't worry, young fingers get better.
Hers take out splinters and can knit a sweater!

Sometimes I hear growls down deep in my tummy.
So I feed it good snacks 'til it stops acting funny.
Our school nurse says to eat good food and exercise a whole bunch too!
She says if you're good to your body your body will be good to you.

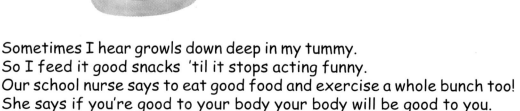

# Dear Parent,

As you know, we mothers and fathers are our children's first and most influential teachers. This colorful volume, *My Favorite Book*, was created especially for your child in that it reinforces, in a positive way, standards of conduct you are teaching in your own home. *My Favorite Book* teaches important lessons in a simple but beautiful manner.

This special gift is made possible through the generosity of local sponsors, people who care a great deal about their community. Their names, addresses and telephone numbers appear in the front of the book. Please give the local sponsors a telephone call just to let them know you received their gift. Giving some indication that you appreciate their generosity not only encourages the sponsors to continue making *My Favorite Book* available to young people, but also models the good manners spoken of in the volume.

Another way to let the sponsors know that their gift has indeed been received, and to send any comments you have, is to use the enclosed SPECIAL SURVEY CARDS. The cards are included only as a convenience. Sponsors do love to hear what children and their parents think of the gift.

Basic standards of behavior are at the core of *My Favorite Book*. Each story encourages the children to do their best and be their best. The *Let's Talk About* sections were designed to help you discuss with your child the important values depicted in each story. Don't forget to look for the *Be Good Bug* in each illustration. We all want our kids to "catch" the *Be Good Bug!* As the children become familiar with the stories they can also make a game of connecting the objects in the front of the book to the appropriate story.

We all know the best thing we can do is give our children time, so reading *My Favorite Book* with your child or helping with words as your child reads and talking about the values in each story is a great activity! We hope this volume will prove helpful to you as you continue to instill in your children the positive character traits that will remain with them throughout life.

# The Stories

**Good Manners** – Character begins with simple civility, and civility begins with developing good manners. The key component of good manners is respect. Respect for individuals is the beginning of civilized behavior. This story points out that simple good manners means respect for others.

*Values: Respect for others, using basic good manners*

***Suggested Family Topic:*** *Talk about how you show respect for others in your daily life. Stress saying "please" and "thank you." This might be a good time to give the sponsors listed in the front of* My Favorite Book *a telephone call to let them know that your child received the volume and to say thank you.*

**Making the World Better** – In this story we honor our elders and we also demonstrate the importance of a respect for the natural world by connecting the work that farmers do with our being able to have food to eat. Of course the key character trait is responsibility, for this character trait is one of the building blocks to good character education.

*Values: Responsibility, respect for the natural world, respect for elders*

***Suggested Family Topic:*** *Talk about some of your responsibilities. Discuss the role of your childrens' grandparents in your life and in their lives.*

**The Hero** – In this story of a boy's bravery and knowledge of emergency procedures, we are able to demonstrate the value of help within the community. Our reliance upon the local community is reinforced by the very method of distribution of *My Favorite Book*, that is, through the generosity of local sponsoring businesses. To have heart is to know the right thing and then to risk doing it. And yes, our hero Jeremy still has to clean his room!

*Values: Bravery, responsibility, and knowledge of emergency procedures.*

***Suggested Family Topic:*** *Talk about people in the community who have helped your family. Use this time to fill out the thank you cards to the sponsors of the* **My Favorite Book** *program.*

**Friends** –We know how important friendships are to youngsters of this age, therefore it is critical for them to begin to understand the nature of healthy and positive friendships. We have used this story to highlight the traits of compassion, respect, patience, honesty and thoughtfulness.

**My Family** -The value of a loving family reaches across all cultural boundaries. The young person in this story loves his family very much. The point is made that even close friends can become like family. The importance of language is also brought out as we make the point that Bobby's parents have learned English well and that Bobby is learning words in both English and Spanish. Both parents are cast in a warm light. An important lesson about familial love is charmingly taught through the family pet, Pancho. Even though he gets into trouble, he is still loved.

*Values: The importance of family and of familial love and acceptance, the importance of heritage and tradition, the appreciation of cultural diversity, the appreciation of our nation and its freedoms.*

*Suggested Family Topic: Tell some favorite family stories. Talk about your family roots. Use this opportunity to teach your child the Pledge of Allegiance.*

**How I Got In Trouble** and **Be Good To Your Body** - Sometimes the simplest lessons are the hardest to teach. Learning to follow rules is essential for the health and well being of our children. When a person in authority, such as a parent or guardian, formulates a set of rules, it is important for the child to obey them. Rules can also pertain to the concept of personal health. The beginning of any drug education program should define for the child the concept of "poison." This lays the foundation for effective learning later on. This clever story and the attendant poem reinforce the value of good health, the dangers of gateway drugs, as well as the importance of being safe by following the rules set out for us.

*Values: How following the rules can keep us safe, the definition of poison and the dangers of alcohol and other drugs. The importance of a healthy mind and a healthy body.*

*Suggested Family Topic: Talk about the specific rules in your home concerning harmful substances. What are some of the rules you follow in your daily life? What kind of exercises can you do as a family?*